TABLE OF CONTENTS

Novel-Ties® are printed on recycled paper.

Copyright © 1984, 2004, 2013 by LEARNING LINKS

For the Teacher

This reproducible study guide to use in conjunction with the novel *Fahrenheit 451* consists of instructional material for guided reading. Written in chapter-by-chapter format, the guide contains a synopsis, pre-reading activities, vocabulary and comprehension exercises, as well as extension activities to be used as follow-up to the novel.

NOVEL-TIES are either for whole class instruction using a single title or for group instruction where each group uses a different novel appropriate to its reading level. Depending upon the amount of time allotted to it in the classroom, each novel, with its guide and accompanying lessons, may be completed in two to four weeks.

The first step in using NOVEL-TIES is to distribute to each student a copy of the novel and a folder containing all of the duplicated worksheets. Begin instruction by selecting several pre-reading activities in order to set the stage for the reading ahead. Vocabulary exercises for each chapter always precede the reading so that new words will be reinforced in the context of the book. Use the questions on the chapter worksheets for class discussion or as written exercises.

The benefits of using NOVEL-TIES are numerous. Students read good literature in the original, rather than in abridged or edited form. The good reading habits formed by practice in focusing on interpretive comprehension and literary techniques will be transferred to the books students read independently. Passive readers become active, avid readers.

SYNOPSIS

In this novel describing a world of the future, an oppressive government controls the populace. It employs firemen to burn all books to discourage the citizenry from thinking, and has installed four-walled televisions to keep them perpetually entertained. But even this world is flawed. For the nine or ten people a night who attempt suicide, technicians are on call to pump their stomachs.

At the beginning of the story, Guy Montag seems satisfied with his lot in life as a happily married fireman whose job is to burn books. This changes, however, when he meets Clarisse McClellan, a seventeen-year-old girl, and an elderly professor who arouse in him a spark of dissatisfaction with his society and his role in it. Montag begins to read books and what he learns causes him to rebel against everything he has always accepted about his life, his wife, their life together, and his occupation.

Montag and the professor plant books in other firemen's homes in an effort to burn down the firehouses, and with them the censorship they impose. Before they can carry out their plan, Montag is called to a final burning: ironically, it is the burning of his own house. His wife reported his collection of books. While trying to resist the assignment of burning his own house, Montag is goaded into turning the fire hoses on his own Captain. Now he is not only a deviant, he is also a murderer.

Montag, as a political refugee, escapes the lethal hunt of the "Hound," a mechanical beast used to track dissenters. He travels to the countryside where he meets and joins a secret, but growing, group of wandering book lovers who hope to restore a rational society by preserving the world's great works of literature for posterity.

AUTHOR INFORMATION

Although Ray Bradbury was best known for his science-fiction novels, he was also a prolific writer of short stories, plays, poems, and children's books. Bradbury was born in 1920 in Waukegan, Illinois. He and his family moved to Los Angeles when he was a teenager. Here, Bradbury attended high school and received the last of his formal education. His interest in the genre of science-fiction was evident during these high school years: he founded *Futura Fantasia*, a quarterly magazine.

Never intending to go to college, Bradbury took on a succession of odd jobs after graduation to support his writing. His early career as a writer was far from glorious: although he sold his first short story at the age of twenty-one, he wrote for pulp magazines from 1941–1945 under a pseudonym.

As a brilliant writer of science fiction, Bradbury predicted man's conquest of the moon and space in his early writings. Yet, for all of his interest in the future, it was ironic that Ray Bradbury refused to use most modern conveniences. Although many contemporary writers today compose strictly on a computer, Bradbury remained devoted to his manual typewriter. He never learned to drive an automobile, nor did he ever fly in an airplane. His preferred mode of transportation was a bicycle.

Ray Bradbury died in 2012 at the age of ninety-one.

PRE-READING ACTIVITIES AND DISCUSSION QUESTIONS

1. Preview the book by reading the title and the author's name and by looking at the illustration on the cover. What do you think the book will be about? When do you think it takes place? Have you read any other books by Ray Bradbury?

2. The genre of science fiction is narrative based on the application of science and technology to imaginary situations. The genre deals either with events that have not yet happened or with events that will probably never happen. It can be set in the future, the past, or another dimension. With your classmates, discuss examples of science fiction that you have encountered in books and in films.

3. With your classmates discuss whether the role of government is primarily to be the leader of its constituency or to reflect the will of those it governs? Find examples of governmental action that reflects each role.

4. What might a government do if it wanted to exact complete submission and quench creative thought from its people? Where and when has this been done by governments? Describe the measures that were taken.

5. Is there any relationship between the literature that exists within a society and the degree to which it can be considered civilized? How might the number and quality of libraries relate to the degree of culture and exchange of information? What might happen if a society lost its written history?

6. Does the growing popularity of electronic books threaten the existence of books in paper and libraries in general? Do you think that the civilized world requires traditional libraries and books in paper format?

7. **Cooperative Learning Activity:** Work with a group of your classmates to create a list of works of literature that you think are essential to Western civilization. Tell why you think each is important. Compare your responses with those of other groups.

8. What happens to an individual who rebels against the government in a dictatorship? What might an individual do to survive if rebellion is impossible?

9. What is censorship? Does a government agency or a community have the right to censor literature? Explain your point of view and debate with someone who holds the opposite opinion. Are you aware of any type of censorship in your community? Are you aware of any governmental attempts at censorship?

10. Create a list of those elements in our society that you think make us a civilized people. What do you think would happen if any one of these elements were removed?

Pre-Reading Activities and Discussion Questions (cont.)

11. Have you read any science-fiction books or seen any films that are in this genre? Did any of them create an imaginary world or predict the future for humanity? How much of these books or films were based upon present knowledge in order to predict the future?

12. What is propaganda, and how do governments use this technique to manipulate the opinions of their people? What kinds of propaganda do we face from government, private companies, schools, and the media?

13. Does the medium of television encourage creative thought or passive thinking? Give examples of specific television programs to support your opinion. In what ways could a government use television to manipulate the lives of its citizens?

14. Does the computer and the internet encourage creative thought or passive thinking? Give examples of specific apps and programs to support your opinion. In what ways might a government use the internet to manipulate the lives of its citizens or its enemies?

PART I — THE HEARTH AND THE SALAMANDER

Vocabulary:
I. Draw a line from each word on the left to its definition on the right. Then use the numbered words to fill in the blanks in the sentences below.

1.	gorged	a.	sense of sight; visual
2.	wafted	b.	mixed feeling of fear, wonder, and reverence
3.	awe	c.	ate greedily until full
4.	refracts	d.	moved or carried lightly through air
5.	imperceptible	e.	having to do with the sense of smell
6.	illuminated	f.	made bright with lighting
7.	optical	g.	dull; unemotional; impassive
8.	olfactory	h.	bends or turns from a straight course
9.	stolid	i.	not easily perceived by the senses or the mind

· ·

1. Standing before the great waterfall, we were filled with an immense sense of
   _____.

2. The long hallway was _____ by four large lamps.

3. The forgery was undetected because there were _____ differences between it and the original.

4. The _____ expressions on the faces of the jury did not reveal whether they found the defendant innocent or guilty.

5. The scent of roses _____ through the cool night air.

6. When you have a cold, your _____ sense is impaired.

7. I had a stomach ache after I _____ myself with food at our Thanksgiving dinner.

8. A lake in the middle of the desert is probably a(n) _____ illusion.

9. Because water _____ light, it is difficult to retrieve a coin from the bottom of a swimming pool.

Part I — The Hearth and the Salamander (cont.)

II. Use the context to determine the meaning of the underlined word in each of the following sentences. Then compare your answer with a dictionary definition.

1. She <u>mourned</u> for her dead mother.
    Your definition _____
    Dictionary definition _____

2. Her sad expression reflected her <u>melancholy</u> mood.
    Your definition _____
    Dictionary definition _____

3. In letters to the local newspaper, people complained about the <u>odious</u> smell coming from the recycling plant.
    Your definition _____
    Dictionary definition _____

4. The band director addressed the <u>cacophony</u> in the music room by raising her hands for silence.
    Your definition _____
    Dictionary definition _____

5. The <u>serenity</u> of the old hotel relaxed us after the long trip.
    Your definition _____
    Dictionary definition _____

6. There are laws which prohibit the <u>exploitation</u> of children as laborers.
    Your definition _____
    Dictionary definition _____

7. The teacher's explanation <u>clarified</u> the difficult instructions.
    Your definition _____
    Dictionary definition _____

8. The <u>ritual</u> of cleansing one's hands is performed before prayers are spoken.
    Your definition _____
    Dictionary definition _____

9. The carpenter had a <u>proclivity</u> for working with wood even after he retired.
    Your definition _____
    Dictionary definition _____

Part I — The Hearth and the Salamander (cont.)

Questions:

1. Notice the quotation at the beginning of Part I: "If they give you ruled paper, write the other way." What do you think this quotation means? How does it relate to the book?

2. Why are the salamander and the phoenix the professional symbols of the firemen? (You may use a standard dictionary to help you find the answer to this question.) Do you think these are appropriate symbols? Explain.

3. What do the numerals "451" represent?

4. In Montag's world, what kind of creature has replaced the usually gentle firehouse dog of our society? What makes this creature so sinister? Why do you think the author has it menace Montag?

5. How is Clarisse McClellan different from the other young people in her society? Explain using evidence from the story. Why does she constantly ask Montag to observe, to taste, to smell, and to touch things in the world around him?

6. How is Montag affected by the event that occurred at 11 North Elm and the woman to whom it occurred? What has happened in this story so far to prepare the reader for this reaction?

7. The television walls have made Montag and his wife into strangers. What else contributes to their alienation from one another?

8. After working on Mildred, the machine operator tells Montage that "we got these cases nine or ten a night." What does this reveal about the emotional stability of the populace? Why do you think this society has become so violent?

9. Montag realizes that all the firemen are mirror images of himself. What does he mean? What characteristics do they have in common?

10. How did the government of this society gain control over its people?

11. How did Beatty describe the decline of civilization that led to the public's taste for mediocrity in the media? What did Beatty mean when he said that "a book is a loaded gun"? What was the basis for his opinion?

12. What does Beatty mean when he says, "We're the Happiness Boys, the Dixie Duo"? What kind of happiness does he espouse? Could Mildred be considered happy according to this definition?

Questions for Discussion:

1. If one were to rebel against Montag's society, what form might this rebellion take?

2. Based upon what you have read so far, what warnings about our own world are suggested by Ray Bradbury in the society he depicts?

3. What might be the equivalent of a book burning in a world where all books have been digitalized?

Part I — The Hearth and the Salamander (cont.)

Literary Devices:

Ray Bradbury is an author whose prose reflects the imagery of a poet. Examine the literary devices he employs to thoroughly appreciate his style as a writer.

I. *Symbolism*—A symbol in literature is the use of an object or an idea to represent an entire set of ideas. In this novel the central symbol is that of fire. What does it represent in Part I of the novel? Notice what it represents at the end.

_____

_____

What do light and dark represent? Skim back over Part I of the novel and list the many allusions to brightness and shadow, and those characters who seem to possess these qualities. Add to this chart as you continue to read the book.

Light	Dark

Part I — The Hearth and the Salamander (cont.)

II. *Irony*—A situation is ironic when it becomes the exact opposite of what is intended. What is ironic about the job of fireman in Montag's society? What other examples of irony can be found in the novel?

_____

_____

III. *Simile*—A simile is a comparison of two unlike objects using the words "like" or "as." For example:

> He wore his happiness like a mask and the girl had run across the lawn with the mask.

What is being compared here?

_____

What does this reveal about the individual?

_____

_____

IV. *Metaphor*—A metaphor is an implied comparison between two seemingly unlike objects. For example:

> Her face, turned to him now, was fragile milk crystal with a soft and constant light in it.

What is being compared?

_____

What is the effect of this comparison?

_____

_____

V. *Alliteration*—Alliteration is the repetition of the same consonant sound at the beginning of words in order to produce a desired effect. For example:

> [The train] slid soundlessly down its lubricated flue in the earth.

What sound is repeated?

_____

What effect does this produce?

_____

Writing Activity:

Imagine you are Guy Montag. You have spent your entire life fearing books and then burning them. Now you are questioning your society. Write a journal entry describing your inner turmoil.

PART II — THE SIEVE AND THE SAND

Vocabulary: Use the context to determine the meaning of the underlined word in each of the following sentences. Compare your definition with a dictionary definition. Then use the underlined words to fill in the blanks in the sentences that follow.

1. The actor stood alone in the center of the stage to deliver his <u>monologue</u>.

   Your definition_____

   Dictionary definition _____

2. Diabetes is an <u>insidious</u> disease; you can have it without feeling any of its symptoms.

   Your definition_____

   Dictionary definition _____

3. The traitor Benedict Arnold was held in <u>contempt</u> by the American patriots.

   Your definition_____

   Dictionary definition _____

4. He <u>manifested</u> his courage when he walked into the burning building.

   Your definition_____

   Dictionary definition _____

5. The <u>beatific</u> smile on the boy's face gave no hint that he had just stolen a cookie.

   Your definition_____

   Dictionary definition _____

6. The colonists rebelled against the <u>tyranny</u> of the King of England.

   Your definition_____

   Dictionary definition _____

. . . .

1. The victim showed his _____ for the kidnappers by going on a hunger strike.

2. Governments that rule by _____ are often despised by their own people.

3. The cabinetmaker _____ his skill when he produced a perfect replica of the antique dresser.

Part II — The Sieve and the Sand (cont.)

4. We were not aware of the _____ work of the embezzler until we noticed the empty shelf in the safety deposit box.

5. Standing apart from the other actors at the front of the stage, the main character revealed his inner feelings in a well-spoken _____ .

6. Her _____ smile made her look like an angel who was incapable of committing the crime.

Questions:

1. When Faber is first introduced in the novel, why is he so critical of himself and pessimistic about the world? Why is he then willing to become Montag's mentor?

2. What is the action of sand through a sieve? Why is "The Sieve and the Sand" an appropriate title for this section of the book?

3. Why are the characters on the television screen called "The Family"? What purpose are they supposed to serve in this society? What is the role played by the "White Clowns" seen on television?

4. Why does Faber think that the people, not the government, brought the present state of affairs upon themselves?

5. How do Montag and Faber plan to save their society? Do you think this plan might succeed?

6. Why do you think Faber chose the Book of Job from the Old Testament as his first selection to read to Montag? What relationship is there between Montag and the biblical Job?

7. What advice is Faber offering Montag when he makes the statement, "If you hide your ignorance, no one will hit you and you'll never learn"?

Questions for Discussion:

1. Montag makes the following comment to Faber: "Maybe they're right, maybe it's best not to face things, to have fun." Do you agree or disagree with Montag's statement?

2. Why do you think the author indicated that the entire world was at war?

3. Do you agree with Faber that the acquisition of wisdom requires the taking of risks?

4. What media counterparts exist today that might satisfy the need for violence in large segments of the population? Do you think these media counterparts satisfy or incite violence?

5. Do you think revolution is inevitable in an oppressive society? What contemporary evidence can you provide to support your conclusion?

6. Why do you think Mrs. Phelps cries in response to Montag's reading of the poem "Dover Beach"?

Part II — The Sieve and the Sand (cont.)

Literary Element: Characterization

Compare and contrast the characters of Faber and Captain Beatty in a Venn diagram such as the one below. Write about their common characteristics in the overlapping part of the circles.

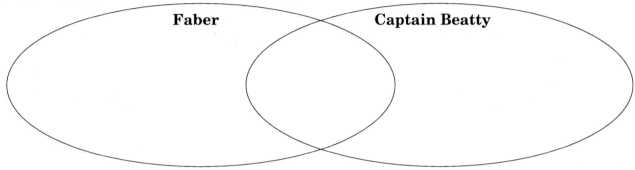

Faber   **Captain Beatty**

Literary Devices:

I.   *Cliffhanger*—A cliffhanger is a device borrowed from silent serialized films in which an episode ends at a moment of heightened tension. In a book it is usually placed at the end of a chapter to encourage the reader to continue on to the next part.

What is the cliffhanger at the end of Part II?

_____

What do you predict is going to happen to Montag?

_____

II. *Allusion*—Allusion in literature is a reference, usually brief, to a presumably familiar person or thing. Why do you think Faber alludes to the legend of Hercules and Antaeus? What lesson might his society learn from this Greek myth?

_____

_____

III. *Symbolism*—What do you think Montag's fever symbolizes?

_____

_____

Writing Activity:

In another book of your choice find an example of prose or poetry that you feel is particularly moving or important. Share it with others in your class as an example of text that should never be destroyed. In a short written essay explain why you think this writing should be preserved and read by successive generations.

PART III — BURNING BRIGHT

Vocabulary: Synonyms are words with similar meanings. Use the context to choose the best synonym for the underlined word in each of the following sentences. Circle the letter of the word you choose.

1. Without my prior instruction, the control panel of the rocket will be <u>incomprehensible</u> to me.

    a. violent   b. unintelligible   c. reasonable   d. amusing

2. The grandparents were exhausted after trailing after their two-year-old grandson who was in <u>perpetual</u> motion.

    a. continual   b. sporadic   c. imperceptible   d. chaotic

3. To survive the effects of a first-degree burn it is <u>vital</u> to have immediate first aid.

    a. foolish   b. effective   c. unusual   d. necessary

4. Everyone on the road should be <u>wary</u> of drivers who weave from one lane to another.

    a. doubtful   b. cautious   c. insecure   d. aggressive

5. To take a picture, you must look through the viewfinder and click the shutter <u>simultaneously</u>.

    a. quickly   b. clumsily   c. repeatedly   d. concurrently

6. The war will continue indefinitely as each side is committed to <u>avenge</u> past killings.

    a. repay   b. repress   c. condone   d. instigate

7. The government worried that people marching with anti-government placards might <u>incite</u> a riot.

    a. demote   b. assist   c. induce   d. inform

Questions:

1. How does Montag feel as he burns his own house? Why do you think he feels this way?

2. Captain Beatty has always told Montag not to face a problem, but to burn it. Explain what becomes ironic about this statement.

Part III — Burning Bright (cont.)

3. What revelation does Montag have about Beatty after he kills him? How does Beatty's ability to quote from literature actually foreshadow this understanding of his character?

4. What does Montag learn about the excessive cruelty of young people as he is making his escape?

5. How does Montag escape from the Hound?

6. What does "a glass of milk, an apple, a pear" represent for Montag?

7. Montag comes upon a group of men who welcome him to their campfire. How is the fire of the camp different from any fire Montag has ever know?

8. How will Granger's group try to preserve civilization? In what way is their role similar to that of the monks during the Dark Ages? According to Granger, what will have to happen before there can be another Renaissance?

9. Why is Montag's capture depicted on television even though he escaped?

Questions for Discussion:

1. According to Bradbury, the following authors needed to be preserved: Byron, Machiavelli, Ghandi, Jefferson, and Lincoln. Why do you think Bradbury selected these authors? What others would you add to the list?

2. Why do you think the government permits the existence of the procession of men along the railroad tracks?

3. Why do you think Granger proposes that a mirror factory is the first order of business in a new society?

4. Why do you think the author depicts the total destruction of the city at the end of the book?

5. Do you think the author wants the reader to believe that Montag will be happy with the book people? In general, would you say that this novel ends on an optimistic or pessimistic note?

Literary Devices:

I. *Allusion*—Read the poem "The Tyger," by William Blake. Why do you think Bradbury alluded to this poem when he titled Part III, "Burning Bright"?

_____

_____

_____

_____

Part III — Burning Bright (cont.)

II. *Simile and Metaphor*—What is being compared in the following simile and metaphor:

> There it lay, a game for him to win, a vast bowling alley in the cool morning. The boulevard was as clean as the surface of an arena two minutes before the appearance of certain unnamed victims and certain unknown killers.

_____

_____

_____

What mood do these figures of speech create?

_____

_____

Writing Activity:

Near the end of the novel, Bradbury compares man to the phoenix. Write an essay to describe how man is similar to this mythical bird. How might this provide hope for the future?

CLOZE ACTIVITY

The following excerpt is taken from Part III of the novel. Read it entirely before going back to fill in the blanks. Afterwards, you may compare your language with that of the author.

Half an hour later, cold, and moving carefully on the tracks, fully aware of his entire body, his face, his mouth, his eyes stuffed with blackness, his ears stuffed with sound, his legs prickled with burrs and nettles, he saw the fire ahead.

The _____[1] was gone, then back again, like a winking _____.[2] He stopped, afraid he might blow the _____[3] out with a single breath. But the _____[4] was there and he approached warily, from _____[5] long way off. It took the better _____[6] of fifteen minutes before he drew very _____[7] indeed to it, and then he stood _____[8] at it from cover. That small motion, _____[9] white and red color, a strange fire _____[10] it meant a different thing to him.

_____[11] was not burning. It was *warming*.

He _____[12] many hands held to its warmth, hands _____[13] arms, hidden in darkness. Above the hands, _____[14] faces that were only moved and tossed _____[15] flickered with firelight. He hadn't known fire _____[16] look this way. He had never thought _____[17] his life that it could give as _____[18] as take. Even its smell was different.

_____[19] long he stood he did not know, _____[20] there was a foolish and yet delicious _____[21] of knowing himself as an animal come _____[22] the forest, drawn by the fire. He _____[23] a thing of brush and liquid eye, _____[24] fur and muzzle and hoof, he was _____[25] thing of horn and blood that would _____[26] like autumn if you bled it out _____[27] the ground. He stood a long long _____,[28] listening to the warm crackle of the _____.[29]

There was a silence gathered all about _____[30] fire and the silence was in the _____[31] faces, and time was there, time enough _____[32] sit by this rusting track under the _____,[33] and look at the world and turn _____[34] over with the eyes, as if it _____[35] held to the center of the bonfire, _____[36] piece of steel these men were all _____.[37] It was not only the fire that _____[38] different. It was the silence. Montag moved toward this special silence that was concerned with all of the world.

POST-READING ACTIVITIES

1. Notice the copyright date at the beginning of the book. How long ago was this book written? Are any of Bradbury's warnings relevant to today's world? Have any of his forecasts about violence come to pass? How do you think this book might have been different if it were written at the beginning of the Internet age as opposed to the beginning of the television age?

2. Do you think the people in today's society who criticize or censor literature are great readers? On what do you think they base their pronouncements? Is there any justification for the censorship of books and other media?

3. *Fahrenheit 451* is a book whose drama is heightened by a multiplicity of sharp contrasts. Explain how the following contrasting characters and images play against one another.

light	—	dark
fire	—	ashes
city	—	country
Faber	—	Beatty
Clarisse	—	Mildred

   Find other examples of contrast within the novel.

4. An author can convey ideas by manipulating the reader's sympathies within the novel. Consider the following situations from the novel and tell which ones evoked sympathy and which ones evoked indifference. In each case indicate what the author's message might be:

   - Mildred's suicide attempt
   - Clarisse's disappearance
   - Beatty's death
   - the stranger killed instead of Montag
   - the death of the woman at 11 Elm
   - the city's demise
   - the isolation of the book people

5. Discuss why Bradbury chose the medium of science fiction to convey his ideas. What strong social statement is the author making about the future of humans in a technological world? What does he feel society and its individuals must do to prevent destruction of the species? If Bradbury were to write a similar book today, what additional menaces might he warn against that have become evident since the book was written?

6. Select another book of science fiction that is set in the future (e.g., *1984, Brave New World*) and compare the worlds depicted in each. Did each author recognize the same hazards in modern civilization? Did each view the future optimistically or pessimistically?

Post-Reading Activities (cont.)

7. This modern classic contains some elements of traditional folk legend: the characters are clearly good or evil, there is a message or moral, and it may be argued that the book ends happily. Substantiate this point of view with specific examples or debate this interpretation with classmates.

8. An author of fiction gives the illusion of a whole world from the presentation of carefully selected fragments. It is interesting to consider, after reading the entire novel, what elements of life the author has chosen to omit. Tell why you think each of the following was not included in the novel, and then list some additional omissions.

   • romance

   • references to the arts of painting, sculpture, and dance

   • young children

   • details about other countries in Montag's time

   • specific details about the workings of government

   • specific details about Clarisse's fate

   Choose one of these omitted elements and write about it as though it were part of the book.

9. View the film version of *Fahrenheit 451*, a classic by the French filmmaker Jacques Truffault. What parts remain true to the original? What parts have been changed? How do you like the film as a whole? Do you like it more or less than the book?

10. View Michael Moore's film *Fahrenheit 911*, a work that is critical of the George W. Bush presidency. What is the main theme of this film and why do you think Moore referred to Bradbury's book title in the title of his film?

SUGGESTIONS FOR FURTHER READING

* Adams, Richard. *Watership Down*. HarperCollins.

Asimov, Isaac. *Foundation Trilogy*. HarperCollins.

Butler, Samuel. *Erewhon*. Penguin.

* Christopher, John. *The White Mountains*. Simon & Schuster.

* Golding, William. *Lord of the Flies*. Penguin USA.

Huxley, Aldous. *Brave New World*. HarperCollins.

* L'Engle, Madeleine. *A Wrinkle in Time*. Random House.

* Lowry, Lois. *The Giver*. Random House.

Miller, Walter M. *A Canticle for Liebowitz*. Random House.

* Nelson, O.T. *The Girl Who Owned a City*. Random House.

* O'Brien, Robert C. *Z for Zachariah*. Random House.

* Orwell, George. *Animal Farm*. New American Library.

* _____. *1984*. New American Library.

Rand, Ayn. *Atlas Shrugged*. New American Library.

_____. *The Fountainhead*. New American Library.

Wilder, Thornton. *Three Plays: Our Town, The Skin of Our Teeth, Matchmaker*. HarperCollins.

Some Other Books by Ray Bradbury

Dandelion Wine. Random House.

The Halloween Tree. Random House.

The Illustrated Man. Random House.

The Martian Chronicles. Random House.

October Country. Random House.

Something Wicked This Way Comes. Random House.

* NOVEL-TIES Study Guides are available for these titles.

ANSWER KEY

Part I

Vocabulary I: 1. c 2. d 3. b 4. h 5. i 6. f 7. a 8. e 9. g;   1. awe 2. illuminated 3. imperceptible 4. stolid 5. wafted 6. olfactory 7. gorged 8. optical 9. refracts

Vocabulary II: 1. mourned–felt or expressed sorrow 2. melancholy–sad or full of sorrow 3. odious–foul or evil 4. cacophony–harsh sound 5. serenity–calmness 6. exploitation–utilization for profit 7. clarified–made clear 8. ritual–formal ceremony 9. proclivity–inclination or tendency

Questions: 1. This suggests that people have to find their own way and not submit blindly to authority. This is what Clarisse was trying to show Montag. 2. The salamander is a mythical reptile said to live in fire. The phoenix is a mythical bird fabled to live 500 years that burns itself on a funeral pyre and rises from the ashes to live another cycle of years. Answers to the last part of the question will vary. 3. The numerals "451" represent the temperature at which paper burns. 4. Unlike the usually gentle firehouse dog in our society, the firehouse dog in Montag's world is a mechanical Hound, programmed for violence untempered by human emotion. The Hound seems to sense the change in Montag even before he is aware that his sympathies are changing. Answers to the last part of the question will vary. 5. Unlike other young people in her society, Clarisse experiences the world with all of her senses and she appreciates nature. She wants Montag to do this also, instead of living a robot-like existence. 6. Montag is horrified at the cruelty of this book burning. Through Clarisse he has begun to understand the importance of books and the need to question what he is doing. 7. Other elements besides the television wall contributing to the alienation between Montag and his wife are the radio earphones, the drugs, and the driving at a suicidal pace. 8. Much of the population is unhappy with its existence and is trying to repress unhappiness through drugs. Answers to the last part of the question will vary. 9. All of the firemen have sunburnt faces, charcoal hair, fevered eyes, and soot-colored brows. Montag is beginning to realize that they are evil and as long as he is a fireman, then he is evil, too. 10. The people relinquished their intellectuality in favor of mass culture mediocrity; thus, rendering themselves incapable of governing themselves. 11. In describing the decline of civilization, Beatty stated that every minority needed to be satisfied, all culture reverted to mediocre mass media, school standards relaxed, and people lost interest in all that was intellectual. According to Beatty, a book could question the status quo, and people would begin to question their world. This might end "happiness" and bring about revolution. This was the cause of mankind's unhappiness and the wars of former times. 12. Beatty means that the firemen and their world bring superficial happiness. It requires total acceptance, the absence of all pain, and no questioning. Answers to the last part of the question will vary.

Part II

Vocabulary: 1. monologue–long speech by a single person 2. insidious–doing harm secretly 3. contempt–condition of being despised 4. manifested–showed plainly 5. beatific–blissfully happy 6. tyranny–oppression; 1. contempt 2. tyranny 3. manifested 4. insidious 5. monologue 6. beatific

Questions: 1. At first, Faber believes that he is not sufficiently rebellious, but feels it is too late to change the world. Helping Montag rekindles his desire to act toward change. He becomes Montag's mentor because in doing so he no longer feels utterly helpless and hopeless. 2. Sand flows through the mesh in a sieve without interruption. This mirrors Montag's attempt to learn the entire Bible in which he retains almost no information. 3. The nuclear family, as well as the extended family, have disappeared in Montag's world and the television "Family" has become its mechanical replacement. The "Clowns" serve the purpose of satisfying the lowest common denominator of taste for violence. 4. Faber thinks that the people allowed this to happen to themselves without being sufficiently critical, by not rewarding intellectuality, and by accepting mass culture. 5. Montag and Faber plan to print books and plant them in firemen's houses. This would sow seeds of suspicion and undermine the entire corrupt fireman structure. Answers to the second part of the question will vary. 6. Despite major hardships, Job continued to believe in God, to work toward that which he believed was morally correct. Faber knows that he and Montag will meet many dangerous stumbling blocks, but that they must continue to believe in the virtue of their actions. 7. Faber wants Montag to question everything, to admit what he needs to know so that he will learn. He needs to take risks.

Part III

Vocabulary: 1. b 2. a 3. d 4. b 5. d 6. a 7. c

Questions: 1. As Montag is in the process of burning his own house, he is literally numb with disbelief. Answers to the second part of the question will vary. 2. Montag's entire life, here symbolized by his house, has become a problem. It is ironic that Montag is following Beatty's instructions to burn it. 3. Only after Beatty's death does Montag realize that Beatty wanted to die. He had been a living lie—only someone who was a reader of books could have been able to quote so widely and so well. 4. Montag understands the excessive cruelty of young people in his society as he makes his escape: they would have run him down on the highway as part of their night's sport. 5. Montag escapes from the Hound by washing his body in the river, putting on Faber's clothes, and dousing his body with liquor; thus, obscuring his own body smell from the Hound's detection. 6. A glass of milk, an apple, and a pear represent that which is pure and natural to Montag. They represent the best in the old order which preceded his technological society. 7. The fire of the men is warm, inviting, and friendly. It is constructive rather than destructive as were the fires in Montag's prior world. 8. In order to save civilization, each person will bear a book in his memory. The books will be stored in this way until the time is ripe and it is possible to translate them into print again. In a sense, the monks during the Dark Ages made their monasteries the repositories of literature in places that would be safe from marauding barbarians. Granger believes that there can be no Renaissance until the current society completely destroys itself. 9. Montag's capture is televised because the government wants the people to believe that its power is infallible. A society dependent upon technology cannot admit imperfection.